Get Out of Your Own Way

"Success Handbook Series"

By
John R. Calabrese

Get Out of Your Own Way

"Success Handbook Series"

Copyright © 2021 by John Calabrese

All rights reserved. Reproducing this work in any form whatsoever without permission in writing from John Calabrese, except for brief passages in connection with a review, is strictly prohibited.

Contact us at
Growth Is a Decision
www.Growthisadecision.com
John@growthisadecision.com

ISBN: 978-1-952281-40-2 - Hardback
ISBN: 978-1-952281-41-9 - Paperback
ISBN: 978-1-952281-42-6 - eBook

Table of Contents

Preface 1
Introduction 5
Chapter One: Your Superpower 9
Chapter Two: Your Story 21
Chapter Three: Influences, Curses, and
Programming 35
Chapter Four: How to Manage Your Emotions 63
Chapter Five: How Health Plays a Role in
Your Success 75
Chapter Six: Stuck 95
Chapter Seven: Things You Can Do 105
Chapter Eight: Some Additional Things
to Consider 123
Closing Words 135
Bio 151

Preface

At the time this book is being released, the world is dealing with the COVID-19 pandemic. My intent for this book is to assist people with staying positive, overcoming challenges, and taking charge of their lives.

The perspectives given in this book have come from teaching martial arts for over 35 years and training in martial arts for over 40 years. I have also formally trained in personal development information from a western approach for well over a decade within groups like the Global Information Network and other sources.

What I have found is that the information taught in martial arts and personal development is similar but expressed differently. Experiencing these multiple viewpoints has given me a unique perspective.

I've had to work through many big challenges in my life using my training in martial arts and personal development. So, this book comes from a place of knowing what it feels like to work through hard things.

My goal for this book is to help you move your life continuously forward by providing a concentrated, condensed, and useful view of the information I have learned from too many teachers, perspectives, and experiences to list.

There are so many great teachers and resources on the subjects discussed in this book. There are sources out there devoted solely to specific topics discussed here, and I recommend finding the ones that resonate with you.

Authors I would recommend include Napoleon Hill, Kevin Trudeau, Esther Hicks, Dr. Joseph Murphy, Bob Proctor, Wayne Dyer, and Bob

Doyle, to name a few of the many great resources out there.

I'll share perspectives, but the principles have been around for thousands of years. The information is organized in a flow that can be easily followed, along with personal insights.

Introduction

We all want to lead a successful life. I define success as having good relationships, health, financial security, and quality of life, although how you determine success is up to you.

We can be our own worst enemy or our own best friend. Often, we have qualities or attitudes that do not help us to succeed. How we think and believe can hold us back from having what we want. We have no idea that we are doing this. We will be exploring how and why we do this and what to do about it throughout this book.

People often get in the way of their success. This can be called "self-sabotage," which describes the result, but we are going to be exploring the causation and how to address it.

Our conscious mind directs 30 percent of our actions. The other 70 percent is directed by our subconscious mind. So much attention is given to the 30 percent that we can see, but the subconscious mind is a better place to focus our attention and effort since it is the cause of 70 percent of our actions. Even if we say we consciously want something, what our subconscious mind believes and what we feel subconsciously will most likely produce the result.

Our brain is similar to a large and powerful computer. Dr Joseph Murphy authored several books about the conscious and subconscious mind, he calculated that it would take a computer the size of a city block to do the things the brain can do. The brain is programmed by our own thoughts, spoken words, experiences, and outside influences. We are born with some software from our DNA. The programming can be added to, changed, or removed. Gaining control of the programming will change the outcome of our lives and determine our level of success.

It is important to note that the brain and the mind are two separate things. The brain is a physical organ in our skull that runs the body. The mind is energetic; it is outside the body and influences the brain. This is a general description of a complex concept that I will explore in greater depth within this book.

There are underlying forces at work affecting our lives. It is important to identify them in order to have more deliberate control of them. Yes, it is even possible to put them to work to improve our lives.

I would highly recommend you read my first book, *You Are the Common Denominator in Your Life*. The information discussed within it will give you a helpful basis of understanding for this book.

There are questions at the end of each chapter as well as blank pages for you to answer them. You can also use them to write some notes. I encourage you to do this because it will help you to get more out of the book.

Chapter One

Your Superpower

"We all possess a superpower. Sometimes it helps us get what we want in our lives and sometimes it brings us things we don't want."

Our Superpower

We create our own reality. Many people are unaware of this and do not consciously use their superpower. How you think creates your reality. You control how you think. You have the power to create your life. In this chapter and throughout this book I will explain how your superpower works in more detail.

We have both a mind and a brain, we will discuss both throughout this book. Your brain is like a computer, collecting data that it operates off of. Our brain also operates the body, perfectly and without any conscious effort. We do not have to think about beating our heart or any other internal bodily function. These are automated systems that run like clockwork. The brain regulates the body chemically as well. We would have a difficult time fathoming all the work our brains are doing at any given moment. The brain is always gathering new information to operate from; beyond that is the mind's domain.

We learn through repetition; we develop neural pathways. Learning also causes the growth of new gray matter. This all causes habits to be formed so we do not have to relearn things. You have heard the expression "It's like riding a bike." Our neural pathways are similar to a preprogrammed action, something we can do without consciously thinking about it. You do not have to think about tying your shoes. You couldn't forget how to write your name if you tried. We literally program our brains and form habits. These habits can be good habits that lead us to success. They can also be bad habits that cause us to harm our chances of reaching the success we are pursuing. This connects with several other concepts we will be discussing throughout the book.

It is important to understand that you have both a brain and a mind: two totally different things. The brain is a physical organ in the skull. The mind is energetic and resides outside of the skull. It has also been called your "higher consciousness." Our brains are influenced by the mind.

Another feat our brain performs is that it is a transmitter and receiver of frequencies. The frequencies transmitted by our brains are determined by our predominant thoughts, emotions and feelings. The frequency with which we think these thoughts and the emotional intensity we attach to them are what gives them power, and this leads to the actions we take. We create our reality with our thinking. Earl Nightingale said, "We become what we think about most of the time"; even Albert Einstein spoke about this saying "The world we have created is a product of our thinking". Buddha said "All that we are is a result of what we have thought. The mind is everything. What we think, we become."

What we receive from this is our reality. This why it is so important to maintain positive thoughts and emotions as much as possible. Speaking positively is important as well, but our emotions are a key factor. We ask for what we want vibrationally through the emotions and intention behind our thoughts and words. That is why it is important to think about what you want and feeling good. We have more control of our lives than most might think. Negative energy can be used to our advantage—it has enormous power, but only if we use it for clarity of what we do not want, keeping our focus on the outcome we do want. Using this incorrectly, becoming focused on the negative outcome, can be a pernicious and a disempowering experience. I recommend working on the positive thoughts and emotions and staying away from negativity as much as you can. We will discuss how to regulate your emotions further in a later chapter.

I think giving some examples of what I mean will be helpful. Have you ever been in a situation where you wanted a specific outcome, and you felt so happy and confident in what the outcome would be? Even when it looked unrealistic, you never wavered in your knowledge of how things would turn out—and then it happened just as you felt it would?

On the other hand, have you ever taken the opposite approach to something you wanted, doubting you would get the outcome you wanted? You would think about all the ways it could go wrong, you'd talk to others about it not working, and worry constantly only to create that or a similar result? You created a self-fulfilling prophecy. These are simple examples of how your brain creates your reality through how you feel and what you think mixed with emotion and belief. So, as you can see, the brain runs our bodies, keeping us physically operating.

Even knowing this information does not mean you are safe from your negative thoughts. It really comes down to your state of mind. When you feel good, you think and speak from a positive place; conversely, when you feel bad, you tend to think and speak negatively, and that leads to negative situations that match the frequencies you are putting out.

The way we think and feel engages the Law of Attraction, also known as the Law of Resonance. This natural law states that like attracts like. Our situations and circumstances and the events in our lives will match our thoughts, words, emotions, and beliefs.

Using our minds and brains, we create our lives through the frequencies we transmit and receive. We have the choice to create and transmit frequencies that match what we want to manifest. If you don't deliberately engage in this practice, you will still be creating what happens in your life. The problem is that you will be unaware of what you are creating until it becomes your reality. You have an amazing superpower; use it deliberately to create the life you want to live. Just as with Spider-Man, "With great power comes great responsibility." Use it well.

Get Out of Your Own Way

What were your takeaways from this chapter?

What action steps can you take?

What points do you need to reflect on?

Chapter Two

Your Story

"Tell a different story, even if it is not likely. Make it go your way with your thoughts, words, and belief. Your belief is the only belief that matters. Do this and watch how your life changes for the better."

Everyone has a story. There is the "how your day is going" story, the "money woes" story, "how your life is going" story, and a whole host of other stories people tell. Most often, it is a horror story. Their story is about all the challenges and bad things that have happened to them. This story will be experienced over and over until they start to tell a new story.

Rarer is hearing the story of the challenges they faced and how they used them to reach for success. The story you tell is your choice. Many times, people have a well-rehearsed story. Often, people tell us how they feel based on how the story is told. I understand that when bad things happen, you cannot just slap a happy-face sticker on it and call it a happy thing. You experienced it, felt it, and own it. What is done cannot be undone, but you can change how you view it. This will require effort and a new perspective.

Tell a different story, even if it is not likely. Make it go your way with your thoughts, words, and belief. Your belief is the only belief that matters. Do this and watch how your life changes for the better.

The story you tell is the life you live; it shows where you may be headed and, based on which specific emotion you're feeling, can determine which health problems you may face as a result. We will discuss how your emotions affect your health later in this book.

There is a connection to how you think, feel, and speak. When you constantly think thoughts of worry, you are literally bringing your worrisome situation into fruition. By focusing all your energy on a bad outcome, you create it. It is the equivalent to praying ceaselessly for your negative thoughts to come true. When you expect something to happen, it generally does.

Why not think about something positive and see what happens? As long as you're expecting something negative that seems unrealistic, expect something great that some people may say is unrealistic. There is enormous power in expecting something, positive or negative. The problems lie in the fact that most people expect the worst and are generally not surprised. Your feelings have a lot of power in creating what happens in your life. Emotions felt intensely or a predominant feeling have an amplifying power on attracting what you want, in accordance with the Law of Attraction.

Thoughts lead to feelings, which are then expressed and clarified through words. The thoughts and the emotions are broadcasted by the brain and bring in situations that align with that broadcast. If you think about future successes and focus on what you want, you are more likely to succeed—it will just be a matter of time before it happens.

This is where most people go wrong. More often than not, they focus on things not going the way they want—on failure. My advice is to try to have more thoughts about good outcomes than bad ones and keep increasing those good thoughts.

It is not a zero-sum game. Expect to win and use any losses to fuel your next win.

Have you ever noticed what dominant sports teams do? They expect to win, and they do the right things in preparation to give them the indomitable spirit that they bring to their game. If they lose, yes, they get very angry, they may throw their helmets and utter some words not suitable for TV—then they turn it into fuel to win their next game. Thinking about losing is like praying ceaselessly to have things go bad, complete with strong emotion and plenty of examples in the past to verify you are right to expect the bad outcome. Everyone has power over their situations. The problem is not everyone knows this, or if they do know it, they are not using the power they have. The ones who do know it and use it deliberately to create their lives focus on what they want not what they don't want.

What do you do with the memories of negative experiences you have collected since you were a child? You're bound to have plenty of them, along with some negative neural pathways to deal with as well.

There are many methods and techniques designed to release these trapped negative emotions. TFT (Thought Field Therapy), BEST (Bio Energetic Synchronization Technique), I-Ching Systems instruments and other energy-clearing modalities can help you to clear blocks that are holding you back.

One thing you can do is meditate, going back to each situation and look at it objectively as an adult. View these experiences from a new perspective. See how they may have been helpful to you in some way in your life or at least understand them differently than you did back then, being magnanimous and forgiving to yourself and those involved and understanding about why you and they did what they did. You must forgive them and yourself. That does not mean you have to apologize to anyone, just feel it in your heart and move on. You can do this through meditation, reflection, and contemplation. Don't let your past define your future.

As a martial arts Grandmaster friend of mine says, "The past is good for two things: information and entertainment."

We will explore more ways to defuse trapped memories and emotions throughout the book.

The main point is to take power over your story and tell it in a way that helps you rather than hurts you.

You can tell where you are at by what you say: the topics you bring up and your attitude toward them are part of your story. I was walking through the grocery store when I heard a man ask a woman how things were going, and she responded, "Same stuff different day." This woman was bored and held a bleak view of the future. By telling this story, she was also strengthening that program in her brain, making it more likely to continue. If you constantly tell your tale of woe, it will continue to repeat itself over and over in your life. You are creating your life's experiences by the story you tell yourself and others.

Tell a different story, even if it is not true yet. Express what you want to happen. If you get excited talking about something you want, you energize your desire for it and your willingness to go after it. You will get into alignment, or "in the zone." Talk about the great things that you have experienced or will be experiencing in the future. Plant the right seeds, get the right crops.

Now, if you talk about worrisome, fatalistic, or unwanted outcomes, that is what you will get: more worrisome, fatalistic, or unwanted outcomes. That is what those seeds grow into. The story you tell is programming your subconscious mind, which directs so many of your actions. Your brain does not know the difference between imagination and reality, so it will believe everything you tell it, good and bad. Get it to believe your awesome hopes and dreams and you are likely to make them come true. The same is true if you tell yourself or others your worst nightmares—you are likely to experience them. You choose to program yourself with your dreams or your nightmares; it's ultimately up to you. The most important story is the one you tell yourself.

Your story is also expressed through your patterns, habits, and what you fight against. Fortunately, these are all things you control, and you have the ability to change. Take the time to listen to the story that you tell others and ask yourself, is that what I want? Because that is what you will most likely continue to experience.

Spend a few days listening to how people start their conversations and see how many people start by complaining about how their team lost the game or how bad traffic or the weather was this morning. You will be scared straight, listening to how negative people can be without a clue they are setting themselves up for more of it.

Tell a different story. Even if it is not true, make it true with your thoughts, words, and belief. Your belief is the only belief that matters. Do this and watch how your life changes for the better.

What story do you tell?

Tell the story you want to experience!

John R. Calabrese

What were your takeaways from this chapter?

What action steps can you take?

John R. Calabrese

What points do you need to reflect on?

Chapter Three

Influences, Curses, and Programming

"Create your beliefs deliberately, and believe in yourself. You choose what you believe and do not believe."

Every day, we face many forms of both positive and negative influences. How we respond to those influences is what matters. Identifying the influences and not accepting their negativity is key. This chapter will provide insights that will be helpful in doing this.

False Beliefs

We create our false beliefs. These can be the reasons we give as to why we are not where we want to be. Sometimes it something that was said to us or something we experienced that we created a belief from. We care too much about what other people think and take those thoughts on as our own beliefs. Sometimes the worst ones can come from the things we come up with and say to ourselves.

Our thoughts produce our words, and with time and repetition, together they become our subconscious beliefs. We don't even know what we have created until we see the same results happening over and over. Listening to the way you talk and watching for patterns will give you an idea of what subconscious beliefs you are operating from.

Your thoughts, words, and beliefs must be congruent to get the outcomes you want.

Henry Ford is known for the saying "Whether you think you can or you think you can't either way you're right, it's the thinking that makes it so."

Your thoughts produce your words, your words aid in producing your beliefs, and your beliefs influence your actions. An example of this would be if you are taking a test and you believe you are going to pass, you will be more motivated to study and become more prepared to pass the test. Just as if you think you will fail, you will not be as motivated to study. Why would you bother to try extra hard if you are planning on failing? It would be a waste of time since you believe you are going to fail anyway.

Create your beliefs deliberately and believe in yourself. You choose what you believe or do not believe.

Here is a true story that shows how if you give up your belief to cater to what someone else believes, you will fail. Fortunately, I refused to believe what I was told and held strong in my own belief.

I wanted to manifest something big, so I said to myself "I will manifest a five-digit windfall of cash." So, I thought about it and came up with an idea that I would sell a six acre plot of land I had in New Hampshire just off the Connecticut River. I had tried to sell it before, but I was going to make it happen. When I called my realtor, she said people were looking at the land for sale there, but no one was buying. Perfect—here was my challenge. I priced my land a little lower than the competition's and put my realtor to work on selling it.

My part was to employ my mind and my belief that I would sell the land and achieve my goal. I used many techniques and protocols to condition my mind to hold this belief strong and use the Law of Attraction.

After seven days, I received two cash offers. Now I was waiting to hear when we could close, giving me a quick victory. This is where things got a little messy. My realtor called to inform me that there was a problem with the title. The land had been given to me in lieu of a payment that was owed to me, and I did not do a title search when I received the land. There was an issue from 1945 with a bank that was no longer in business. The realtor told me that she did not see how this could be resolved. That was her belief, not mine. I will admit I initially felt like I just got punched in the stomach—it was a big disappointment.

This is where my self-awareness kicked in. My next thought was "somehow this is going to work out to my advantage." Remember, this is where most people would listen to the professional and quit. They would take on the belief that they would not be able to fix the situation. I called my lawyer and he got to work on it.

Yes, I was investing more money into this impossible situation by hiring a lawyer because I was holding strong in my belief that this was all going to work out to my advantage. When you are in that mindset and you only see the outcome you want, you know it will happen at the perfect time, in the perfect way—although the perfect time may be different than the one you had in mind. This is another reason people give up: because it is not happening on their timeline. The Universe, God, or Source Energy (depending on your belief system) knows that the perfect time is not merely your preference.

When I started this project, I did not need the money for anything specific. When manifesting money, it is important to know how much money you want and what you will do with it.

Well, six months later I had an investment opportunity, and I needed that money. I committed to it with only faith that the money would show up. The next morning, my lawyer emailed me that my title was cleared, and I was free to close that week. There were many lessons learned from this experience, but the big one was to trust myself and what I knew and not to adopt someone else's beliefs just because they were the professional in that area. The other lesson was just how important knowing what you're going to do with it is. When you have a reason for wanting it your desire is stronger. It is easier to picture it, you add emotions, and it feels more real. I was put on hold for six months until I figured that out, and then it was delivered right away.

It took six months of holding strong in the belief that everything would work out to my advantage, and it played out in an amazing way—just as I needed it, I received it.

How many false beliefs are you operating from? Looking at things from multiple perspectives can give you some clarity.

Self-Sabotage

What is self-sabotage? Have you ever said or done something—or not done something—that derailed your plans and then asked yourself, "Why did I do that?" Most of the time you have no idea why. It is very possible you placed in your subconscious mind the order to bring about a failure. Often it is based on false beliefs that you allow to reside within you. It could be based on past failures or the feeling you are not worthy of that level of success. These stories loop in your thoughts and are programmed into you. These programs can run deep within you, but using the suggestions in this book, you can in time replace them with more beneficial programs.

This is like a computer virus. Remember, your brain is like a computer. There is a saying about computer coding: Garbage In, Garbage Out (GIGO). You feed your mind and brain information all day. This comes in the form of your internal dialog, the thoughts you think, your beliefs, and your opinion of yourself. There are external influences as well. Know that your brain takes in everything in your environment, twenty-four hours per day, seven days per week. This includes while you sleep. So, if you fall asleep while watching TV, you still hear the programs and commercials. They go directly to your subconscious mind because the conscious mind is unable to push back on them. The commercials can be the most harmful since they are designed to influence you.

Change your thoughts, words and beliefs to getting what you want and you will be in the driver's seat heading toward your successes. Do this and self-sabotage will not be in your way.

Negative Self-Talk

Self-talk is your internal dialogue. For example, you keep thinking of the worst-case scenario about a situation in your life, playing it out in your head with all the horrific details. Self-talk is also when you speak these words aloud to yourself. Have you ever heard someone say "I am so stupid" after making a careless mistake? They just asked their subconscious mind to help them to do more stupid things. Your subconscious mind takes everything you say literally as fact and as an order to be carried out. Tell it good things about yourself and what you truly want, not what you do not want. Saying those things to others is also especially harmful. Now you have conspirators adding to your demise—you have made an agreement with them to work toward a negative result.

Be aware of your self-talk. Is it positive or negative? If you have a habit of negative self-talk, catch yourself and, over time, replace it with positive self-talk. Use positive self-talk to energize your goals and how you feel.

Curses

There are many types of curses, and I am not talking about voodoo. In this context, I would call a curse any thoughts, words or actions that influence you to have doubt or other negative thoughts and emotions that bring about situations, circumstances, and events that you do not want. We are going to cover several ways we curse ourselves.

Based on this description of what a curse is, who casts curses on you? The real answer is: you do, although others can influence you in this. There are other types of curses, but that is not what we will be going into here today.

When someone pessimistically states to you that they do not think you can do something, they are cursing you, provided you let them. When someone shares negative thoughts about their opinion of you personally, what you are doing or what you are attempting to accomplish, they are cursing you. These can very easily be the people who love you the most, just trying to be helpful but having the opposite effect. In their eyes it does not look realistic, and they are saving you from a failure. The danger here is that you can be led into doubting yourself. Ultimately you are the one cursing yourself because you have the choice to accept this or reject it. If you accept it and have doubt, you lose momentum and desire and your energy fades—checkmate, you just lost to the curse. If you reject this, you are empowered and increase your ability to succeed.

Here is a clear example of how dangerous what we are calling a curse can be. Let's say you smoke cigarettes, and your spouse says to you ceaselessly, "If you don't stop smoking you will get cancer and die." You hear "You are going to die" over and over again. They paint a graphic picture of how it will happen in great detail. The fact that they say it is one thing, but the repetition with pictures included can imprint it in your mind. You remember in pictures and learn through repetition. You create what you see in your mind, and this can lead you to visualizing what they said to you. Can you see how dangerous this can be? Had they taken a different approach like telling them they wish they were healthier, and they wanted to see them live a long time. Adding quitting smoking would be really helpful in giving them more years together. Focusing on the outcome you want not what you don't want, painting that picture is a better approach.

Sometimes the best of intentions can disempower and limit the person you are trying to help.

There is a martial art throwing technique called the "over the hip" throw. This technique flips the other party over so that they land in front of you. (You have probably seen this in many fight scenes on television and at the movies, they use it a lot.) If you were to try to hold them back as they fell to soften their landing, they could injure their back. You have to let them go so they can land correctly, avoiding injury on their own. Learning how to fall is an extremely empowering experience. The fear of falling is one of two fears we are born with. Overcoming a fear that is hard wired in your DNA that you were born with. Would you want someone to stop you from experiencing that so they felt better about throwing you to the ground? What a disservice that would be, robbing you of that experience. Trying to help them is like saying they can't do it on their own. It may come from a caring place, but it is still wrong. People, even people who care about you the most, can say or do things to influence you into a negative mindset.

Often, the primary offender of casting these curses on you is yourself. Yes, you may be casting curses on yourself without ever really knowing what is going on. You are getting in your own way. Every time you accept any negative influence, you accept a curse. Every time you say you cannot do something; you are cursing yourself. Every time you think a negative or disparaging thought about yourself, you are cursing yourself with it. These thoughts generally come from unguarded self-talk or programmed thought patterns from previous experiences. These stories you play out in your mind can be extremely dangerous.

There is a famous experiment that illustrates the effect of negative influences. You take two identical plants and give them the same amount of water, sunlight, and care. The only difference is in how you talk to them and the energy you throw toward them. One plant you are mean to, throwing hate and negativity toward it. The other you express love and positive energy toward. The one you are kind to will flourish; the one you throw negativity toward will wilt and die. This is true with people too. You can read about this in the book *The Secret Life of Plants* by Peter Tompkins and Christopher Bird.

Tell a child or an adult they are a failure enough times and they are likely to become one. Although children are very impressionable, adults are also greatly affected because they may have had experiences in their life that could be used as evidence of the truth of any given statement. Constant criticism, whether it is meant to be constructive or not, will do major damage to the recipient and can harm their self-image, self-esteem, and confidence.

Have you ever heard of "gaslighting" someone? This is a method used to destroy or control someone's thinking. You tell someone lies until they give in and believe them. Their heads are filled with false narratives, fake news, and agendas. You can view this as a form of propaganda, repeating lies until they are believed. You see this a lot in politics and the media.

One example of this is if a person comes into work feeling fine. Everyone at work tells them they look extremely sick and keeps asking them if they are ok, saying "you look horrible, do you need to go home?" They will eventually go home sick. Or you convince them they are losing their minds by telling them complete falsehoods until they don't know what to believe anymore and accept the false story you are telling them about things they didn't actually say or do. This is an example of knowingly cursing someone.

How do you avoid the curses or the accepting of doubt in yourself and your goals? Remember, you choose to accept or reject these influences. Generally, no one is trying to curse you, including yourself. Others may have no idea of the effects they are causing. The best step to take is to keep your thoughts to yourself until you have accomplished your objective—then you can tell others. You may tell certain people whom you know will support and encourage you in what you're doing. If it is a public situation, then just limit your conversation and stay away from the subject. A more direct approach is to confront their opinion, then reject it and hold fast in your knowledge that you are making the best decision.

You should make sure you are not being delusional, though. When I was a teenager in the early 1980s my teacher Grandmaster McGee pointed out the calligraphy hanging on the wall in the martial arts school and was explaining their meaning. One Mind, Indomitability and Fame were among them. In talking about fame, he told me, "Don't fall into a fantasy or delusion" and "It's OK to live a fantasy life, just don't get into a fantasy mind."

I have heard this point said by others over the years in different words but such an important point. I took that as you should walk your talk and that I should have high aspirations to live an amazing life, but I also must be willing to do the work needed to accomplish those aspirations. A simple example of this is when you want good health, but you eat an unhealthy diet, you do not exercise, you do not get enough sleep, and you go out drinking every night. This will not produce good health. Your thoughts and actions must be in alignment with what it will take to be healthy. If they are not, you would be *doe chi*, which is a Korean martial arts term that means *drunk by one's own idea*. I was taught this early in my martial arts training. My teacher had me spin around in circles until the room appeared to be spinning. He asked me what I saw, and I replied that the room was spinning. Then he asked a couple of other students what they saw, and they said the room was still. I got the point.

Believe in yourself and make decisions based on what you know and feel. Don't let other people's thoughts and feelings become your thoughts and feelings. This is a choice.

Acceptance

There is a phenomenon where people will believe or do things just to gain acceptance from others. People seem to crave acceptance and will ignore facts and common sense. This can be used against you in many ways.

I was watching a TV show called *Brain Train*. They brought ten people onto a large ship where they had three white boards on easels. Each board had a thick black line on it. The first board had a line about sixteen inches long; the second board's line was the same size exactly, and the third line was shorter at about ten inches.

Everyone was lined up and asked one at a time which line didn't match the others, but nine of the participants had been told in advance that they should pick the first board. The first nine people picked the first board, even though it was clearly the wrong answer. The tenth person, who was unaware of what was happening, went last. She looked and said "I want to say 3 but even though it doesn't make sense, I'm picking the first one since everyone else has, so there must be something I don't know."

She clearly went against her own judgment in an effort to fit in. You could see her wrestling with her decision the whole time, because picking the first board made no sense at all.

The show ran several other similar scenarios with the same results. When I watched this, I thought *how can you do that*, but it shows how far people will go to fit in and gain acceptance. Don't fall victim to this. Do not let others do your thinking for you—it is very disempowering.

As you can see, there are many ways we are influenced by others. Our responsibility to ourselves is to keep our minds sealed against these negative influences and instead own our own thoughts. How you feel about yourself is what's most important.

Comparing

When we look at people who have done great things and aspire to do the same, that can be a good thing, but when you compare yourself to others thinking they are better than you, that is a problem.

No one is as cool as they seem. People lead with their strengths and don't show you their weaknesses. Everybody has issues; facing our own individual challenges is part of life and no one is exempt. You know both your strengths and your weaknesses; you see only their strengths. What winds up happening is you compare your weak spots to their strengths, and that is not fair to yourself. They are not as great as you think they are, and you are better than you think you are. Comparing your weaknesses to other people's strengths in not a fair comparison. Be fair to yourself.

Other Outside Influences

Messaging in advertising, the media (including social media), TV, music, and many other platforms will program you to their point of view through spaced repetition. Changing traditional views, social engineering, and a whole host of infringing agendas are put in place through this method. Portray a bad thing in a positive light enough times, and over time, people will accept it. This is what the Nazis did through their propaganda programming.

Be aware this exists and rely on your own independent thinking to decide what you believe or don't believe.

There are many good influences we can surround ourselves with. I am a member of several organizations and clubs that are filled with like-minded people and foster a positive, growth-oriented environment where I have learned a lot of powerful information.

Clubs like Toastmasters can be a great experience. The training and networking opportunities that the Global Information Network provides are very beneficial. Joining an internal martial arts school is a great idea.

Some memberships are more exclusive, like mastermind groups, professional groups, or martial arts groups like the Master Level Teaching Group, where membership is by invitation only and is earned.

What you read, watch, and listen to should be in alignment with raising your vibrations and feeling positive emotions. Take responsibility for everything in your life, including how you respond to negative influences. Keep lots of positive influences in your life to counteract the negative influences you can be exposed to while you continue to limit the negative influences in your life.

What were your takeaways from this chapter?

What action steps can you take?

John R. Calabrese

What points do you need to reflect on?

Chapter Four

How to Manage Your Emotions

"Negative emotions like anger, grief, rage, and worry cause the release of stress hormones, also referred to as death hormones."

Dr. Maxwell Maltz explains in his book *Psycho Cybernetics* that we are born with two fears: the fear of falling and the fear of loud noises. All other fears and emotional responses are learned.

We are emotional beings, and emotions are not inherently bad. Positive emotions are awesome. It all depends on what the emotion is, how intensely you feel it, and how often and long you feel it. Some people can feel an emotion like anger or grief for years.

Positive emotions like joy, love, and laughter can energize you and release many happy hormones like endorphins, serotonin, and oxytocin into your body. This is a great state in which to create or manifest things you want. Having intense positive emotions sustained for long periods of time can supercharge your ability to create and manifest.

Negative emotions like anger, grief, rage, and worry cause the release of stress hormones, also referred to as death hormones; these can weaken you. These emotions also weaken specific organ systems, known to martial arts through the "Five Elements Theory" and Traditional Chinese Medicine (TCM).

Certain emotions cause health issues when experienced repeatedly. When you experience consistent anger, it can negatively affect your liver. Hold on to past issues and the large intestine pays the price. Worry is connected to the stomach—this is why stomach ulcers are often caused by stress and worry. Fear weakens the kidneys and bladder. Have you ever heard the phrase "I was so scared I almost peed in my pants"? According to Qi Gong teachings holding onto a negative emotion for seven years or more makes you very vulnerable to serious health issues. This is based on internal alchemies found in the five elements theory. Whether you understand this or not, it's still going on.

When you are caught up in your emotions, controlling them seems near impossible. Try telling someone who is experiencing a fit of rage to manage their emotions. I can tell you that will not end well. We are emotional beings; it is just what we do. But there are things you can do to regulate these sensations.

First, self-awareness is necessary. You need to recognize what is happening and want to pull free of the negative emotions you're experiencing. It sounds irrational, but when you are in an emotional state, you feel justified to stay in the experience. Have you ever seen someone all twisted up in their emotions and you tell them to calm down? Their response will be something like "You want me to calm down? Did you not see what just happened? Why would I calm down?" Emotions are tricky.

Providing you can get to a place where you want to address your emotions, there are things you can do.

Working out with strenuous exercises can help burn them out.

Qi gong has a set of movements called "healing sounds." There is a specific sound you make as you exhale in conjunction with a physical movement. There is one for grief or holding onto emotions, worry and ruminating thoughts, anger and rage, sadness, and fear. These movements can be done in combinations to amplify the effects. They are not difficult to perform—being willing to let go of the emotions can be the hardest part.

Meditation can be tricky. If you try to enter a quiet place while strong negative emotions are running, you could put yourself in a worse place as you dwell on the issue you are emotional about, looping those thoughts and becoming hyper-focused on how you feel about the issue. Then your internal dialog kicks in to reinforce your negative position. You are now on a runaway train. Moving meditation or meditations that use chanting or mantras may work better in separating you from the emotions you are experiencing.

Acupuncture or acupressure can be very helpful. For example, the meridian point of liver 14 is great for addressing feelings of anger. You basically scrub your bottom right rib back and forth with your forearm.

A similar method would be TFT, or Thought Field Therapy, a method founded by Dr. Roger Callahan. Although Roger has passed away, his widow, Joann, is still carrying on his work. You basically tap on meridian points in a certain sequence to remove entire chains of trapped emotional issues. Many meridian-tapping protocols have been developed from this original system, like Emotional Freedom Technique by Gary Craig, and Quantum Energetic Clearing (QEC) with Lee Beymer who were both students of Roger Callahan.

BEST (Bio Energetic Synchronization Technique), developed by Dr. Milton Morter, is a great method for peeling the onion of trapped emotions.

There are many other release methods like these out there. Find what method feels right for you, but do not keep your emotions bottled up inside you or they will harm you over time.

While we don't always feel good when we are doing challenging things, we may feel great about why we are doing them, and we enjoy the results. Exercising self-awareness of your emotions can help you to connect to your gut more, giving you greater intuition. This is where the term *a gut feeling* comes from. This is the area where your conscious mind and sub-conscious mind intersect.

As you can see, there many ways to help you balance your emotions, even the deep, less visible, trapped emotions and energies. You want to amplify your good emotions and minimize your negative ones. Find the methods that resonate with you and that you find effective but do be aware of your emotions and regulate them as needed.

What were your takeaways from this chapter?

What action steps can you take?

What points do you need to reflect on?

Chapter Five

How Health Plays a Role in Your Success

"What you think and how you feel about your health does affect your health."

Good health starts in the mind. It is an attitude and a mindset. You need to expect to be healthy. Any thoughts counter to this are counterproductive to gaining or maintaining good health.

What you think and how you feel about your health does affect your health. There was an experiment shown in the docudrama *What the Bleep!?: Down the Rabbit Hole* where two groups of people ate chocolate cake. One group viewed the cake as unhealthy and thought it would have a negative impact on their health. The other group loved the cake and had no worries about eating it. Doctors performed medical tests on them with surprising results. The first group had a negative result from eating the cake, just like they thought they would. The second group had a positive response after eating the cake. How do you look at your food? I am not saying cake is good for you, but how you view it does matter.

I heard a story about people on a plane being told that the food they just ate was rotten, and they all felt ill and threw up even though there was nothing actually wrong with the food. So, you can see how what you think matters. Your brain does not know the difference between reality and imagined situations.

I am not a dietitian or nutritionist, and each person reacts to foods differently. We have different metabolisms and needs. Some people gain weight easily where others burn it off quickly. Some people's bodies respond well to red meat; others have an adverse reaction to it. What is right for one person is not right for another, so I will not write from a one-size-fits-all perspective. Educate yourself on the subject; it is up to each individual to decide what is best for them.

How does good health help you to be more successful? The mind and body are intertwined, each affecting the other. If your physical health drops, it weakens your mind and vice versa. It can be difficult to feel good mentally or emotionally when you're dealing with health challenges. Your mental and emotional state influences and creates what is happening in your life.

Mind-Body Connection

There is a constant battle for control taking place between your mind (consciousness) and your body (ego).

Have you ever seen the image of the person with a little devil on one shoulder and an angel on the opposite shoulder?

For our example, the little devil would be your ego, which favors what your body wants. The angel would represent your higher self, or your mind.

Your body seeks protection, comfort, and what makes you feel good in the moment. When you are cold, you want to do things to get warm—this is a good thing. When your body is tired, you want to sleep—again, this is a good thing. Your body even has a sprinkler system to cool you down when you overheat, called perspiration.

An example of when this is a problem is when your mind wants your body to exercise to promote better health, but your body knows this hurts, which it does not want. Your mind knows this is temporary pain to achieve a higher purpose. Higher purpose comes from the mind. Your body is programed to seek safety and comfort. Your mental willpower needs to be able to override your body's influence. Either your mind controls your body, or your body controls your mind. Who do you want to listen to? Being aware that this paradigm exists is a good place to start. Then develop a strong mind by building your willpower. Willpower gives your mind the power to override your body's influence where appropriate. Doing challenging exercises strengthens the nervous system, which the brain is connected to and which in turn connects to the mind. This process strengthens the mind's ability to control the brain and body, making it easier to exercise self-discipline and push yourself mentally and physically, giving you the ability to get the results you want.

The brain and the mind are two distinctly different things. Our brain, as part of our nervous system, is like a computer that runs our body. The mind is energetic and exists outside of our body. It is our higher self. An easy way to understand this is to imagine there was a fire in a building: our brain/body would want to run out of the building and seek safety, while our mind would want to run inside, risking harm in order to rescue others—acting with a higher purpose.

Why does our body react when we think a thought? You think about something sad and your body produces tears, or you're watching a horror movie and think fearful thoughts and your heart races with a rush of adrenaline. Those are some simple examples of the mind and body connection. We think thoughts that lead to emotions that produce a physical response.

Why is health so important to success in life? Without your health, nothing else matters. Mental and physical health are both important. A method of maintaining both is martial arts. I have found internal martial arts like bagua zhang, tai chi, and qi gong to be outstanding styles; they are effective, and you are never too old to do them.

There are both highly strenuous and low-impact approaches to martial arts training.

Strenuous martial arts training can be hard. It can be like making a sword: first you put it in a hot fire, then you place it on an anvil and pound the impurities out of the metal, and then you stick it in water to cool it off. This is repeated until you have a pure hardened blade. That may not sound like fun, but it's the results that make you feel good, not necessarily the process that takes you there. Low-impact training like tai chi and qi gong is a much softer approach that focuses on your chi energy, internal development and understanding the internal alchemies.

Through training, you also develop many traits that are able to be used regularly in life.

These are just a few.

Vibrant Health

Vibrant health is extremely important. Energy flow becomes regulated and balanced promoting healthier organ systems. Your immune system is supercharged, you gain increased range of motion with healthier joints and connective tissue. Having greater range of motion with your body is freeing both mentally and physically. When your body contracts and stiffens, so does your mind.

When you have health issues, they prevent you from feeling good and distract you from focusing on the good things in your life. Be like the Taoist Immortal, which is someone that is fully functional mentally and physically until the day they die. Your mind will stay sharp, and you will still have full range of motion and control of your physical body. This is achieved through internal martial arts practiced over a lifetime.

Confidence

Someone can say they are confident the sun will rise in the morning—that's not the confidence we're talking about here. When you believe in yourself, when there is a risk of failure and you do it anyway—that's confidence.

Confidence comes from believing, then achieving. When you do something successfully, you have increased your belief in yourself, which creates mental momentum. You feel more confident that you can do big things. Through this process, you can see and believe that you can do other things. Repeat this process until your belief in yourself is not limited to specific goals. In martial arts, this momentum comes when a student achieves their next belt rank or reaches a new level of ability in performing a kick or movement. The system of training is set up based on a sequence of achievements that bring the student to higher and higher levels of confidence. Bringing this confidence into their daily life is the goal.

Patience

There are two types of patience. One is your willingness to take your time to focus on a difficult task, not getting upset if you must wait an extra hour or day. The other is when you set a goal and you stay active in its pursuit, over decades if necessary. An example would be going from a white belt to a black belt or rising to the position of master or sifu.

Perseverance

Perseverance is the ability to withstand the most painful aspects of the journey. You're like a Weeble-Wobble: you get knocked down, but you pop right back up. It is your inner terminator; it just can't kill you.

Willpower

Willpower is the willingness to do something difficult when it would be easier not to. For example, you could sit on the couch and watch TV, but to get up and exercise instead requires willpower. It's you launching into action, which requires a burst of energy to get things moving.

Determination

Determination is the ability to keep going through a long and arduous journey. Running a marathon requires determination both in the preparation and in the actual event. If you are looking for a job, then doing that every day all day and stopping at nothing until you find one would be a good example of being determined.

Focus

Concentrated focus and long-term focus are two types of focus a martial arts student develops. There is micro and macro focus, specific and big picture. Long-term focus is aided by patience and determination.

When you work on important paperwork, you can get an intense laser focus on the task at hand. This would be an example of micro-focus. An example of macro-focus is when you pursue a long-term goal that will take years of consistent focused effort to obtain while staying the course to the finish line. Having the ability to draw upon the ability to focus your mind is a valuable skill to possess.

Tempering

Tempering is mental and physical toughness; it is achieved purely outside of your comfort zone, by pushing your body and mind past your preconceived limits. A student does this until it is considered the norm and they love the next challenge. This process is what enables someone to have increased mental toughness to handle the difficult circumstances or challenges they may face in their life.

Self-Belief

Self-belief comes from confidence but is not limited to believing you can or cannot do something. When you have self-belief, you believe in yourself so strongly that temporary defeats do not affect your willingness to persevere toward a goal or outcome.

Empowerment

Empowerment is the fuel for self-belief. It is inspiration and feeling indomitable. When we are encouraged or experience a victory, we are empowered. This is confidence, believing in yourself, and feeling supercharged all rolled into one.

Leadership

Leadership always starts by being able to lead yourself before you can lead others. You start by doing the right things and being an example to follow. As a martial arts student, I expressed my desire to be an instructor and help people. I did not get the response I expected. My teacher said I must build myself up first so I could have something to help them with. A leader can be viewed as guide taking others down a path they have been down many times before.

My teacher's teacher's teacher, a grand master from my lineage, put it this way: "Treat your students like they are your children, treat your teachers the way you would treat your parents, and stay loyal to and follow the dao."

Leadership is seen in what you do and how you care for those you are leading. The consistent example you show and how you treat and relate to those you lead define you as a leader.

There are many more benefits beyond this but I think you get the idea.

Your health is the most important aspect of your self-development. Without good health, you are at a severe disadvantage. It is harder to regain good health once you have lost it than it is to maintain good health. Just because you are not sick doesn't mean your healthy.

There are times where we don't have the money to do the thing we want to do to invest in our health. You may want to eat organic food, but it is too expensive, or you want to buy the best supplements but do not have the money for them, and so on. Do what you can to invest in your health, not everything you do to improve your health costs money. One cost of good health can be time and effort. You may want to make different spending choices aligned with your health.

A great book on health that I highly recommend is *Natural Cures They Don't Want You to Know About* by Kevin Trudeau.

Continuously invest in your health in every way you're able. Invest time, money, and effort into building vibrant health. Choosing a form of exercise and staying consistent with it is one of the most important things you can do for yourself. Form healthy habits that replace old unhealthy habits. Make good health a priority. Having good health is a big objective in having a successful life. Neglecting your health would be an example of getting in your own way.

John R. Calabrese

What were your takeaways from this chapter?

What action steps can you take?

John R. Calabrese

What points do you need to reflect on?

Chapter Six

Stuck

"So, what do you do if you get stuck? The first thing you should do is change the story you are telling about yourself and your situation."

What is being stuck? I read a story a while back about a man who was hiking alone in the mountains far from civilization when he got his foot stuck between two boulders and had to cut his foot off to break free. That is not the kind of stuck we will be talking about, but it does paint a picture of the frustration a person can feel when they are stuck.

One form of being stuck is being trapped in an emotion. Some people get angry and stay that way for years. When you have a thought, a chemical peptide is released that matches what you are feeling. A person can get to a point where their body craves that peptide, and a vicious cycle begins. They will find a way to stay angry. This can be challenging to get out of. You can be addicted to an emotion and you will create circumstances to feel it.

We can become trapped within our own patterns and the way we do things. This becomes your comfort zone, which does not allow any change or growth. Outside of your comfort zone is where all the magic happens. How you think can form patterns. A lot of your responses to things can literally be programed into you and your reactions. Some seem like irrational overreactions; this is called a "trigger."

I have seen this when training students in martial arts. One example I saw firsthand was when I was teaching a multi-school program and I told a student she had made an error. The student got upset, left, and told her main teacher that she was quitting martial arts. I met with her and she said I reminded her of her father, who was especially hard on her. After we talked, she could identify this as a trigger and ultimately wanted to address this as opposed to quitting the class or martial arts. In this example, she was getting in her own way before she reversed course and started to grow instead. She was willing to change a disruptive pattern once she realized what it was. You don't have to live your past—blaze new trails through growth.

It is possible to fall into a funk—not necessarily clinically depressed, but still feeling bad. Anything can cause it. Maybe you lost someone you were extremely close to, maybe you lost your job; you could be having relationship, money, or professional troubles. It could be any combination of things, but the result is that you lose motivation, fall into a bad mindset, and experience low vibrations. Feelings of depression lead you to lack of action. That is when things start going in ways that you do not like. Negative thoughts and situations attract more negative thoughts and situations, leading to a downward spiral.

This can end a few different ways. One is that you hit bottom or a major event happens in your life that is a jolt to the system—a "phoenix rising from the ashes" situation. Another way is that you find the inspiration to get up. At some point you will get sick and tired and want to make a change. Sometimes a person could just be in a place where they cannot make a decision. Usually, fear is the culprit, but it could also be lack of willpower or that they are simply in a confused or overwhelmed place.

So, if you hit bottom, you either bounce or you do not. The best way to bounce is with the self-awareness to see where you are at, take responsibility for it, awaken, and get to work on yourself. Everything starts and ends with you. That being said, start making improvements. If you find yourself 200 pounds overweight, then instead of being overwhelmed, start where you are and you address it step-by-step, not all at once. The first thing you should do is change the story you are telling about yourself and your situation. Look at the words you are using. Use positive self-talk; talk about positive outcomes that will be happening in your life. Then take inspired action with full faith that you will succeed.

Feeling stuck can put you in a very painful place. Remember, you can decide to free yourself and do whatever it takes to find your way back to a better place. Get started with the process of freeing yourself by clearing the obstacles you have accumulated throughout your life. Just get to work on yourself.

John R. Calabrese

What were your takeaways from this chapter?

What action steps can you take?

John R. Calabrese

What points do you need to reflect on?

Chapter Seven

Things You Can Do

"We have so much control over what happens in our lives. That is the good news. Now for the bad news: most people do not understand how to control their lives in a deliberate way and become subject to their programming instead of the thinking that aids them in achieving what they genuinely want."

You have taken in some new information as well as additional concepts and perspectives, so now what?

I would recommend you start by taking inventory of where you are at. See where you truly are, energetically, emotionally, healthwise and where your life is. Don't judge whether it is a good or bad place just identify where you can improve and work on yourself. Never stop working on yourself, it is an ongoing process. Then make a decision as to where you want to be and go there, one step at time, never doubting you will get there.

It is important to understand that everything on earth is subject to natural law and the laws of energy. Atoms consist of subatomic particles of energy. Since everything is made of atoms, everything is made of energy. This means your life will unfold based on how energy operates.

We have so much control over what happens in our lives. That is the good news. Now for the bad news: most people do not understand how to control their lives in a deliberate way and become subject to their programming instead of the thinking that aids them in achieving what they genuinely want.

In order to deliberately create outcomes in your life, you must view, think, feel, speak of, imagine, and be a vibrational match to what you want. You must understand, take full responsibility for, and know that you create everything in your life, even if you cannot understand how or why you could be responsible.

I know it can be hard to accept responsibility for the bad circumstances in our lives. We will talk more on this later in this chapter. The good news is that it is easy to take responsibility for all the good outcomes.

The brain thinks thoughts that turn into words and then actions that give us results. Thoughts come first; everything follows them. Your brain broadcasts them; your predominant thoughts combined with the matching emotions have the most power. The more time you spend thinking about your goals while feeling as though they have already been accomplished, the greater your belief, leaving no room for doubt.

Let us say you are trying to accomplish something big in your life and you have full faith and conviction you will succeed. In this state, you are unstoppable. You put enormous time, effort, and energy into it. Not only will you go the extra mile, you are willing to run a marathon if that is what it takes. There are no limitations because you are energized by your enthusiasm. You are now in a position to succeed.

On the opposite side of things, what if you doubt it will be accomplished and take a sour view of things? You think about all of the ways your goal will not work out. You will not go the extra mile. Not only that, but you would not even go a few extra yards since you do not think it will work out anyway. You will not put in enormous time, effort, and energy because you doubt the outcome, so why bother? The difference between the two examples is that when you have no doubt, you do the things that people with doubt do not do. Those with doubt never give 100 percent, and that is a big reason why they fail.

Let's say you trust your gut. You think it said yes and you tried and failed. The temporary failure you experience is not necessarily a bad thing, provided it does not cause you to quit trying. This brings you to a different place where you can see a better opportunity that you could never have seen from where you were. I am not talking about a physical location, but the situations and circumstances in your life that have changed because of your situation—a shuffling of the deck, if you will. Many times, where you are going is not a straight line from where you are. When we doubt or accept the doubts of others, we do a great disservice to ourselves. We deny ourselves the full opportunity to succeed.

Our brain sees in pictures. When we feed it pictures of failing and reinforce those by telling everyone about it, we are enlisting our subconscious mind to help create that reality. This is not hard math: if you keep a vision of good things in your mind, it helps you to achieve them. If you envision bad things, your mind will help you get those. The first way aids your efforts; the second is you getting in your own way. You control this process whether you know it or not. You choose whether you allow others to influence you, and how you influence yourself.

How do you implement all of this? It seems like a lot of work to manage your thoughts, emotions, words, beliefs, and actions. You are working on your health as well as holding off all the negative people and programming coming at you.

There is a saying in martial arts: "Guard your thoughts, watch your words, and keep your chi." First, make sure your thoughts are positive—be aware of the way you speak because it leads to your actions. Keep your good health and do not waste your life force, or chi, unnecessarily. You could also look at it this way; Guard your thoughts, watch your words and create the life you came here to live.

How you think about something or how you view it determines the emotions that you experience. Do your best to stay in a good place as much as you can, finding more positive emotions to feel, and keep adding more of them. Your emotions will tell the story of where you are, positive or negative. If you are having negative emotions, do what you can to shift them toward better emotions. Be aware of your emotional state. Positive emotions lead you to more positive thoughts and actions, and negative emotions lead you to more negative thoughts and actions.

Next, it's about forming habits and routines that aid you in having an unwavering mindset, keeping your thoughts and words aligned with positivity and not getting sucked into all the negative influences we face on a regular basis. Here are some good habits and routines you can form.

Wake up early and do things to create your positive mindset and create positive momentum going into your day.

Do things like read a positive and inspiring book, which will program your mind with helpful concepts and raise your energetic vibration to draw more positive things into your life. You could also listen to audio books or watch some law of attraction YouTube videos, which will also raise your belief and vibration. Most importantly, think about what you want Live it in your mind seeing it, feeling it and experience it in your mind.

Other activities to start your day with would be meditating, exercising or anything else along those lines that you are inclined to do. This sets the tone of the day. There are many other helpful things you can do so find a morning routine that works for you to set yourself up for a more productive and successful day.

Having done this for many years I can tell you firsthand this will make a bigger difference than you might think.

You could do the opposite and wake up late, get your day started late, feel rushed and stressed while leaving no time to put your energetic and mental armor on. This leaves you vulnerable to falling into a negative state with first challenge that you face. I do not recommend this option.

Doing these positive activities throughout the day and especially before bed is extremely beneficial. What you hear, see, or think before falling asleep will ruminate in your head all night long. Another thing you can do is to say thank you for all the things you are grateful for as you fall asleep. Thanking for things you want but do not have yet can be especially powerful in that it will plant seeds in your subconscious mind. I have found this technique helps you fall right to sleep too. Gratitude is a powerful emotion and highly beneficial to the individual feeling it.

Positive self-talk is a powerful tool to reprogram your subconscious mind. Say positive things to yourself over and over throughout the day and as you fall asleep.

Try playing an inspiring audio quietly while you sleep. You have no resistance when your asleep so the information sinks in more easily.

Trust yourself over the opinions of others. I am not saying not to listen to the opinions of people you trust, just that you should make your own decisions. Everyone has the ability to really know what is right for them. Check your gut—some are sensitive to it, others are oblivious to this sense. You can literally feel what the right thing to do is in the solar plexus area of your body. This is where your subconscious mind and your conscious mind connect. This intuition can be developed through inward development like meditation, qi gong, and other mind-body modalities. If your feeling is in your head, it is generally your ego (body) talking.

I personally recommend martial arts as a big part of your personal development training. Many of the principles of personal development have been taught through martial arts for thousands of years. When I was taught these principles, the wording and methods of instruction were different, but the message was the same. My teacher explained the law of attraction as: you plant corn, you get corn. He told us to "be of one mind" and that we needed to "set our minds" or "put mind in" toward what we wanted to make happen. Those were strong concepts if you truly know what is meant by those statements. We were encouraged not be negative, gossip, blame, or complain. OK, "encouraged" would be an understatement—it was more like a demand that was strictly enforced. Like I said, the methods were different. We were taught how to see things through the principles of Buddhism, Taoism, and Confucianism. We were taught chi energy, the mind, and how energy works back when these ideas were considered pure voodoo or crazy talk, in the early eighties before the book *The Secret* and personal development was as well-known as it is today.

Lao Tzu, the author of the Tao Te Ching, said:

"Be careful of your thoughts because they become your words.

Be careful of your words because they become your actions.

Be careful of your actions because they become your habits.

Your habits become your character and your character becomes your destiny."

Which kind of says it all, don't you think.

Another master taught me an enlightening lesson about doubt during a sword class a few decades ago. You can only doubt three things: you can doubt yourself, you can doubt your sword, you can doubt your enemy.

In other words, you can doubt yourself, you can doubt your method, or you can doubt your goal.

I have learned through martial arts and personal development with teachers like Kevin Trudeau, Esther Hicks, and many others, as well as my self-study and looking at these concepts from a scientific perspective, that it is all congruent: you become or get what you think about most.

Decide where you want to go, start taking steps in that direction, and don't stop. Using the information in this book and any other resources you have, navigate the path and enjoy your accomplishments.

If you want things to change in your life, the change must start with you. I say this often, but you must constantly work on improving yourself.

What were your takeaways from this chapter?

John R. Calabrese

What action steps can you take?

What points do you need to reflect on?

Chapter Eight

Some Additional Things to Consider

Broadcasting

We are constantly sending broadcasts from our brain. We broadcast how we feel and what we want or don't want. The power of the broadcast depends on several variables. The biggest one is how you feel. Your emotional intensity and its duration are also important. Don't let outside influences affect what you are broadcasting or how you are feeling.

Imagine yourself as a transmitter broadcasting out frequencies. Each channel on a radio picks up a different frequency, and what we want is on a specific channel. This means we need to match the frequency we broadcast with the frequency of the radio channel we want. This sounds easy enough, right? But it may require some work getting your thoughts, emotions, words, and actions to align with what you want. This is why it is so important to consistently work on ourselves and have self-awareness to manage our frequencies.

Negative influences can make this more challenging. Only you should be setting your radio dial.

Wave Pool Effect

The wave pool effect occurs when we have been in a negative place but then make a change and start being positive and doing all the right things, yet we still have negative circumstances coming our way. This can sink your battleship (dreams).

Let's say you are in a wave pool, in this example, the waves represent negative circumstances and still water represents positive circumstances. So, you hit the off button for the wave machine, but it takes time for the water to become still. This is where many get discouraged and sucked back into the negative patterns of their past. I have always looked at it like a test of whether I am truly serious about what I am trying to do. It can feel like going through turbulence or as though you are breaking through the atmosphere. Know this exists and ride it out when it occurs.

Language of Success

The language of success isn't really a spoken language: it is how you communicate energetically or vibrationally.

It is about what you think and say and the frequency you are broadcasting. You are constantly broadcasting your thoughts. If they are congruent with what you want, then you are on your way. This means you are vibrating the frequency that matches what you want and it is just a matter of keeping the faith and waiting for it to arrive in your reality. Remember, you get what you truly desire and what you fear the most. When you think or talk with certainty about your pending success and then back it up with inspired actions, that is an example of speaking the language of success.

Negative influences come to us in many ways and can be very harmful to our ability to create the life we want. Self-awareness and the willingness to reject what doesn't serve you is so very important.

Reticular Activating System

Our brain has a reticular activating system, which is a filter for the information that we take in and are conscious of. Your brain takes in and filters billions of bits of information, only allowing the most relevant to reach your conscious mind. Everyone's filter is custom to the individual.

Have you ever learned a new word and all of sudden you see and hear that word everywhere, or you buy a new car and you start noticing that same car everywhere even though you hadn't in the past? This is your reticular activating system at work, making you conscious of what has always been there. It is like your saved favorites on your computer. By only allowing certain information into your conscious awareness, you are prevented from going into information overload. This also means that if you focus on a goal, you will notice opportunities and information relating to that goal. When you deliberately focus on something, it is like adding it to your favorites. This will help you to work with the Law of Attraction to intentionally create the life you want to live. Also, remember that energy flows where attention goes. I hope this allows you to see how your brain, mind, and the law of attraction work together. This works two ways: if you focus on what you don't want, you will see that everywhere too. You choose what you focus on and bring into your awareness. This shows us another reason to be disciplined in what we think about. This is science, not a theory. Work with this and it will give you a new tool to use.

My martial arts instructor would make this point to me back when I was starting out as student: a tree is either growing or it is dying; nothing in nature stays the same, and we are part of nature. You are part of nature and need to keep growing.

This applies to our personal growth. If we are not constantly investing time, money, and energy to improve ourselves, we will slide backward.

Don't Let Others Move Your Mind

Grandmaster McGee would tell me on a regular basis, "Don't let someone move your mind," because when you are reactive you give them power over you. You are at a disadvantage when provoked versus when you act of your own volition.

At first, I understood it to mean not to be drawn into a fight so easily. After thinking about it I came to understand what it really meant was don't let others determine what you think and feel.

It has been said you have about 50,000 or more thoughts a day. You are constantly creating with your thoughts. Are you creating deliberately or are you letting others, or your default programming decide for you?

I hope these insights give you something interesting to mentally chew on.

Get Out of Your Own Way

What were your takeaways from this chapter?

… need this... Can you come back with it?'"[1]

As a father, I do this, as well. If I'm in the car with one of my kids, I'll ask them, "Have you thought about how you would solve that situation?" Then, I'll ask leading questions, to help them figure it out. We need to ask these questions of our young leaders, to help them think things through.

What action steps can you take?

What points do you need to reflect on?

Closing Words

Now that you have this information, what do you do with it? You may have identified things you do (or things you don't do) that are slowing your progress toward the goals in your life.

If you can get your thinking right, the rest will follow. Yes, there are other aspects that are very important, like your emotional state. Your emotions come from how you look at something; they are your response to it. Your thoughts create your emotions. If something bad happens and you don't accept it as bad, you won't have a negative response to it. I know that is not always easy, but neither is dealing with the matching frequency of a negative emotion. People generally find it easier to tell you their tales of woe than to tell you how they feel about the good things happening to them. This is a result of negative programming. Don't be that person! Think and talk about the wins!

Pay attention to how you think, speak, and feel; they are very connected.

Sometimes we pursue an outcome that requires a lot of time and effort and sometimes money. It can feel like you ate an entire box of cereal just to get the prize at the bottom, only to discover after all that time and effort that there is no prize at the bottom of the box. One possible reason is that you may have been doing good things, but your thinking, speaking, emotions, and subconscious beliefs were not lined up with what you were attempting to accomplish. This is why I say your thinking is the most important piece, because everything else comes from a thought.

Or the outcome may have been a blessing seen as a failure at the time but later it was recognized as a blessing. Another is that it may have been part of the journey, which is not always a straight line to where you are going. We discussed this at length earlier in the book. There are many other possibilities, but I would say these are the most common reasons.

We need to constantly work on ourselves. Life is constantly changing, and we need to keep pace. Life can feel like a treadmill that keeps changing speeds, and we need to keep our edge sharp to bring our best to creating the life we want to live.

We have explored many concepts, perspectives, and solutions in this book. None of them are the magic bullet, but all of them work together to help you to tune in the frequencies that get you to the channel of feeling good and receiving an abundance of what you want.

Make working on yourself a habit, constantly becoming better and course-correcting where needed. You literally grow to your goals. Use the tools suggested in this book and find additional methods as well.

I look at it as cross-training. Often when someone is serious about exercising their body, they use a variety of methods of exercise, like combining strength training with aerobics and flexibility training to get better results. It is the same thing with getting your energy right.

You may engage in reading personal development books by authors like Napoleon Hill and Esther Hicks or listening to audio like "Your Wish is Your Command" by Kevin Trudeau and watching videos like *The Secret* and *What the Bleep Do We Know* to train your mind into a positive state.

You can also do energy work to release trapped negative energy, thought patterns, and other blocks. This can be through acupuncture, BEST, TFT, QEC, martial arts, yoga, and so many other modalities.

Here is an easy one to do: daydream about your goals and what you hope to achieve. You can impress the image of what you want on your subconscious mind, which will help you to find a way to make it real—remember, your brain doesn't know the difference between imagination and reality.

All of this will aid you in getting your thinking right. Depending on where you are at and what you are trying to do, I have found certain books, audios, and other methods work better than others at certain points in time. It requires your self-awareness to realize what you need.

Think, speak, and visualize what you want instead of what you do not want, and then take inspired actions. It is not very complicated; it just takes focus and self-discipline.

There are videos drilling down on the subjects discussed in this book on my YouTube channel https://www.youtube.com/channel/UCGSeH3bB_AKzcZhJlpvlW-A/videos Watching these videos would be highly advantageous in conjunction with the reading of this book.

Now identify where you need improvement or what you can take further, and work on that. Then it will be easier to get out of your own way.

We have touched on many topics and concepts that you can employ. Putting them into practice is where you really learn and get results. Good luck on your journey to a better version of yourself and the life you create!

John R. Calabrese

How do you get in your own way?

How can you make improvements on that?

John R. Calabrese

Where are you at right now with the things that matter to you in your life today?

Where were you in relation to those things a year ago?

John R. Calabrese

Where would you like to be one year from now?

Where would you like to be five years from now?

John R. Calabrese

Where would you like to be ten years from now?

Questions are powerful because they prompt you to look for answers. Now create strategies and plans on how you will accomplish the goals you listed above.

Bio

John Calabrese is originally from Chicago, Illinois, and currently lives on the North Shore of Boston, Massachusetts.

Professionally, he is a Master-level teacher in martial arts within a 2600 year-old lineage, as well as a speaker, author, coach, and entrepreneur. With over thirty-five years of teaching experience, he has expanded into the speaking, coaching and literary fields.

John has gone through over 40 years of martial arts training and over ten years of formal training in personal development with the top teachers in the industry.

Learning and teaching are his passions. It is John's belief that learning helps to accumulate knowledge, but to teach and apply knowledge is to transform it into wisdom.

In 2002, along with several other Master-level martial arts teachers, John cofounded Body Mind Systems, a martial arts organization and system. Body Mind Systems training focuses on the complete development of the student and their ability to apply the training and principles in their daily life.

Learning about and training in the use of the mind and energy in martial arts led John to expand his pursuit of knowledge to learning more about the Law of Resonance (Law of Attraction), natural laws, success principles, and their applications in life.

In 2015 John started a speaker, personal development coaching and seminar company called Growth is a Decision (www.growthisadecision.com). This was designed to provide a platform to share valuable perspectives, insights and information that he has spent 40 years learning, living and teaching with as many people as possible.

John R. Calabrese

Growth Is a Decision

John@growthisadecision.com

Visit www.GrowthIsADecision.com

"I feel blessed to have written this book and to have the opportunity to share this information with you. It is my hope that you enjoyed and benefited from its concepts and perspectives."

www.ingramcontent.com/pod-product-compliance
Lightning Source LLC
Chambersburg PA
CBHW072017110526
44592CB00012B/1344